IGNITE
555 Powerful Questions to Spark Creativity

IGNITE
555 Powerful Questions to Unlock Creativity

Inspire Bold Ideas and
Revolutionize Your Business by
Asking the Right Questions to
Spark Creativity and Success

Be.Bull Publishing Group
Mauricio Vasquez

Toronto, Canada

Authors:

Be.Bull Publishing Group

Mauricio Vasquez

First Printing: December 2024

ISBN 978-1-998402-79-3 (Paperback)
ISBN 978-1-998402-80-9 (Hardcover)
ISBN 978-1-998402-81-6 (Ebook)

Table of Contents

Introduction: The Case for Creativity in Business

Asking questions is, has been, and always will be at the heart of creativity. Questions open the door to fresh ideas, uncover new opportunities, and inspire innovative solutions to complex challenges in unique and powerful ways.

Why is asking thoughtful and inspiring questions important for business creativity?

First and foremost, asking the right questions fuels discovery. When you ask thought-provoking questions about your business, your market, or even yourself, you are creating a foundation for innovation. These questions disrupt assumptions, challenge the status quo, and spark the kind of thinking that leads to groundbreaking ideas and strategies.

Questions also serve as bridges. They connect you with your colleagues, your customers, and your partners, showing that you value their perspectives and insights. When you ask the right questions—and truly listen to the answers—you foster collaboration, build trust, and create an environment where creative thinking thrives.

But here's the catch: not all questions are created equal. In business, it's easy to fall into the trap of routine, asking the same surface-level or closed-ended questions that yield predictable and uninspiring answers. Worse yet, failing to act on the answers you receive can stifle creativity and damage trust. Asking the right questions—insightful, open-ended, and intentional—goes far beyond gathering information. It's about unlocking new possibilities and catalyzing innovation.

Imagine this: what if you're holding onto assumptions that are outdated or incomplete? What if your current strategies are based on ideas that no longer align with the needs of your customers, your team, or the marketplace? Without asking the right questions, you risk staying stuck in old patterns and missing opportunities for transformation.

Albert Einstein famously said, "Creativity is seeing what others see and thinking what no one else ever thought." This truth resonates deeply when it comes to business creativity. The right question at the right time can shift perspectives, ignite inspiration, and pave the way for game-changing ideas.

You don't need to spend countless hours figuring out which questions to ask. I've done the heavy lifting for you.

This book offers 555 thought-provoking questions designed to spark creativity, uncover new opportunities, and tackle business challenges from fresh angles. These questions are tailored for business professionals who want to rethink, reimagine, and revolutionize their approach to creativity.

With these questions as your guide, you'll unlock the power of curiosity, inspire innovative thinking, and build a foundation for sustained creative growth. Whether you're seeking to innovate your strategies, redefine your business model, or strengthen your team's creative culture, this book provides the tools you need to move forward with confidence.

Your creative journey starts here. Let's get curious together.

Guidelines for Asking Powerful Questions to Spark Creativity

1. Effective questions are open or focused, depending on the context

Creative questions invite exploration. Open-ended questions spark curiosity and imaginative thinking because they cannot be answered with a simple "yes" or "no." These questions encourage deeper reflection, helping individuals explore possibilities and discover unique solutions.

2. Effective questions stimulate innovative thinking

To drive creativity, your questions should challenge assumptions and shift perspectives. Powerful questions help focus attention on key aspects of a situation that are ripe for innovation, whether it's uncovering opportunities, addressing challenges, or reimagining existing processes.

3. Effective questions prioritize the creative process over individual preferences

Creativity flourishes when questions are asked to inspire others rather than serve personal interests. The goal is to encourage teams, colleagues, or even yourself to think beyond the obvious and explore uncharted ideas, rather than guiding answers toward pre-determined outcomes.

4. Effective questions engage personal creativity

Great ideas often emerge from personal insights. By inviting a personal response—how someone feels about a situation or what unique perspective they bring—you can unlock creative energy. When people connect emotionally to a problem or opportunity, their creative responses are often more authentic and impactful.

5. Effective questions shift focus from problems to possibilities

When stuck in a challenge, creative questions redirect attention from obstacles to opportunities. These questions open the door to forward-thinking solutions, helping individuals or teams envision new outcomes rather than dwelling on what isn't working.

6. Effective questions promote exploration, not defensiveness

To foster an open and creative atmosphere, questions should be framed with curiosity and a non-judgmental tone. Avoid leading with "why," as it can put others on the defensive. Instead, use phrases like "what if" or "how might we" to inspire exploration and collaboration.

7. Effective questions facilitate co-creation over directive answers

The most impactful creative questions empower others to generate ideas rather than steering them toward a particular solution. Creativity thrives in a collaborative environment where participants feel ownership of their contributions. Offer suggestions when needed, but frame them as options, not directives disguised as questions.

8. Effective questions provide flexible terms and options

The questions in this book are uniquely designed to meet your creative needs. Each question includes two pre-determined terms or concepts relevant to the topic, providing inspiration and direction. Additionally, every question offers a blank space for you to insert your own term or concept, ensuring the questions align perfectly with your specific challenges or opportunities. This structure encourages both guided exploration and personalized application.

9. Less is more when asking creative questions

Simple, clear questions often yield the most profound insights. Overcomplicated or multi-layered questions can confuse and stifle creativity. A concise question like, "What else could this be?" or "What's another way to approach this?" can provoke powerful, imaginative responses.

By following these guidelines, you can craft powerful questions that inspire creative thinking, unlock innovation, and lead to transformative business solutions. Remember, the art of asking is as important as the answers it evokes. Each question in this book serves as both a guide and an invitation to explore, rethink, and innovate.

Tips for the Use of this Book

These tips are designed to help you make the most of this book's 555 creativity-sparking questions. By tailoring, combining, and building on these prompts, you can uncover transformative insights and foster innovation in every aspect of your business.

- The chapters are guides, not boundaries: The questions are grouped into chapters based on themes, such as innovation, leadership, or operational efficiency. Use these chapters as a starting point, but many questions can inspire creativity across multiple contexts.
- Start with curiosity and active observation: Creativity begins with listening and observing. Pay close attention to the problem, opportunity, or challenge you're addressing. Consider the emotions, patterns, and insights present in the situation to guide how you use the questions effectively.
- Tailor questions to your specific context: For the best results, adapt the questions to align with your unique business needs, challenges, or opportunities. A well-tailored question has the power to unlock insights that are both relevant and transformative.
- Combine and build for deeper exploration: Creativity thrives on layered thinking. Feel free to combine different questions or ask follow-up questions to delve deeper into challenges, uncover hidden opportunities, and spark innovative solutions.
- Each question offers options for flexibility: Many questions come with two pre-determined terms or concepts to guide your thinking and a blank space for you to insert your own idea. This structure allows for both inspiration and personalization, making the questions adaptable to your specific needs.

- Follow-up questions fuel innovation: One question often leads to another. Don't hesitate to explore further by asking follow-ups to uncover deeper layers of insight or refine your understanding of the problem at hand.
- Use your language, your way: While the questions in this book are crafted for clarity, adapt them to reflect your own vocabulary, tone, or industry-specific language. This ensures the questions resonate with your personal and professional style.
- Keep it simple and focused: Creativity thrives in clarity. Ask one question at a time and avoid overly complex or multi-layered questions. A concise and focused approach allows room for meaningful and innovative responses.

Dear Valued Reader

Thank you for choosing this book to ignite your creativity and inspire innovation in your business journey. Your feedback means the world to me, and I'd like to kindly ask for your support in leaving a review.

As an independent author, I don't have the resources of big publishing companies, so your input is incredibly valuable. It helps this book reach more professionals like you who are eager to transform their thinking and unlock new opportunities.

To share your thoughts, simply scan the QR code below, which will take you directly to the review section on the e-commerce channel where you purchase your book.

Your support will make a significant difference, and I truly appreciate your time and help.

Thank you so much!

Mauricio

Empower Your Journey:
Discover More Tools for Success. Scan the QR Code Today

  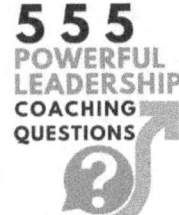 

A Token of Appreciation

Thank you for reading the book "IGNITE 555 Powerful Questions to Spark Creativity".

As a token of my appreciation, I'm sharing a free sample of my book, **"555 Powerful Questions for Coaching, Mentoring, and Leading at Work."**

Scan the QR code below to access your free sample and continue your journey of personal and professional growth!

1. Rethinking Innovation: Beyond the Buzzword

Innovation is more than a buzzword—it's a practical and essential process for driving growth and solving complex challenges. This chapter provides actionable methods like design thinking, lean startup principles, and divergent thinking to uncover opportunities and foster breakthrough ideas in products, services, and processes.

1. What steps can you take to integrate (design thinking/lean startup principles/_____) into your approach to innovation?

2. How might you apply (divergent thinking/brainstorming techniques/_____) to uncover untapped opportunities in your industry?

3. What actions can you take to reimagine your (product design/service delivery/_____) from the customer's perspective?

4. How could you use (prototyping/rapid iteration/_____) to test and refine your innovative ideas?

5. What role can (feedback loops/continuous learning/_____) play in shaping your innovation strategy?

6. How might you challenge (existing assumptions/current processes/_____) to uncover new ways of solving problems?

7. What creative methods can you apply to balance (risk-taking/feasibility/_____) in developing innovative solutions?

8. How can you leverage (cross-disciplinary collaboration/external partnerships/_____) to expand your innovation capacity?

9. What steps will you take to align your (team's creativity/strategic goals/_____) with a culture of innovation?

10. How might you redefine your (business model/service offerings/_____) to better meet evolving customer needs?

11. What actions can you take to turn (constraints/limitations/_____) into opportunities for innovative solutions?

12. How can you measure the success of your (innovation projects/creative initiatives/_____) effectively?

13. What role can (customer empathy/user-centered design/_____) play in uncovering breakthrough ideas?

14. How might you identify and address (gaps in the market/unmet customer needs/_____) through innovation?

15. What specific actions will you take to encourage (open communication/radical ideas/_____) within your team?

16. How can you use (trend analysis/competitive research/_____) to anticipate future opportunities for innovation?

17. What steps will you take to ensure your (experiments/failures/_____) lead to valuable insights?

18. How might you simplify (complex problems/resource-heavy processes/_____) to create innovative solutions?

19. What actions will you take to foster a mindset of (adaptability/curiosity/_____) across your organization?

20. How can you turn (emerging technologies/data insights/_____) into drivers of creative growth?

21. What steps will you take to introduce (structured ideation/design sprints/_____) into your team's workflow?

22. How might you rethink your (value proposition/revenue streams/_____) to stay competitive and relevant?

23. What creative approaches can you apply to overcome (organizational silos/decision-making bottlenecks/_____) in your innovation process?

24. How can you encourage (diverse perspectives/cross-functional collaboration/_____) to generate breakthrough ideas?

25. What actions will you take to ensure that your (innovation efforts/creative solutions/_____) are sustainable and scalable?

26. How might you leverage (past successes/lessons from failures/_____) to strengthen your approach to innovation?

2. Strategic Creativity: Crafting Winning Business Strategies

This chapter invites you to infuse creativity into strategic planning, fostering innovative approaches to gain a competitive edge. These questions are designed to stimulate fresh perspectives, uncover new opportunities, and craft dynamic strategies for long-term business success.

1. What steps can you take to align your (strategic goals/vision for innovation/_____) with the changing needs of your industry?

2. How might you reframe your (long-term objectives/company mission/_____) to inspire more creative strategic thinking?

3. What potential does your (current market trends/customer behavior insights/_____) hold for uncovering untapped opportunities?

4. How can you creatively use your (industry knowledge/data analysis/_____) to redefine your competitive edge?

5. How could you approach your (current business challenges/operational roadblocks/_____) from a completely different perspective?

6. What innovative methods can you apply to address (strategic barriers/market resistance/_____) in your organization?

7. How might you creatively differentiate your (brand value/unique selling proposition/_____) in a crowded market?

8. What actions can you take to transform your (competitive analysis/industry benchmarking/_____) into a breakthrough strategy?

9. How could you leverage (cross-departmental insights/team brainstorming sessions/_____) to refine your strategic plan?

10. What (collaborative opportunities/external partnerships/_____) could add new dimensions to your strategic approach?

11. What creative ways could you use your (customer feedback/market research insights/_____) to shape your strategic priorities?

12. How might you rethink your (customer engagement strategy/value proposition/_____) to better serve your target audience?

13. What (calculated risks/unconventional experiments/_____) can you incorporate to test bold new strategies?

14. How could embracing (failure as feedback/agile thinking/_____) spark innovative ideas for growth?

15. How can you creatively optimize your (time/resources/_____) to execute your strategy more effectively?

16. What (budgeting techniques/alternative funding sources/_____) could enable you to pursue innovative initiatives?

17. How might you adapt your (current strategy/decision-making processes/_____) to remain agile in a changing environment?

18. What (contingency plans/flexible frameworks/_____) can you design to ensure your strategy stays relevant?

19. How can you use (KPIs/innovative metrics/_____) to measure the success of your creative strategies?

20. What (qualitative feedback/data-driven insights/_____) will help you refine your strategy over time?

21. How might you reimagine your (market positioning/strategic goals/_____) to lead your industry forward?

22. What actions could you take to redefine the (future direction/big picture thinking/_____) of your business strategy?

23. How could you creatively integrate (emerging technologies/AI-driven insights/_____) into your strategic planning?

24. What role can (digital transformation/automation tools/_____) play in creating a more innovative strategy?

25. How can you foster (ongoing learning/continuous iteration/_____) to ensure your strategy evolves effectively?

26. What (feedback loops/external inspiration/_____) can you use to refresh and enhance your approach to strategic planning?

3. Leadership with Imagination: Inspiring Creative Teams

This chapter helps leaders inspire creativity within their teams by cultivating an innovative culture. These thought-provoking questions aim to guide leaders in fostering collaboration, nurturing imagination, and unlocking the collective creative potential of their organizations.

1. What actions will you take to enhance your team's (collaborative spirit/innovative mindset/_____) this week?

2. How can you create opportunities for your team to share (bold ideas/unconventional solutions/_____) more openly?

3. What steps can you take to balance (structure/flexibility/_____) in fostering creativity within your team?

4. How might you encourage (risk-taking/experimental thinking/_____) without fear of failure?

5. What (approaches/tools/) can you use to recognize and reward (creative contributions/innovative solutions/) in your organization?

6. How can you use (storytelling/inspirational leadership/_____) to motivate your team to think beyond traditional boundaries?

7. What creative approaches can you apply to resolve (conflicts/creative blocks/_____) within your team?

8. How can you redefine (team roles/organizational goals/_____) to maximize creative potential?

9. What steps can you take to provide (psychological safety/openness to ideas/_____) for your team's creative processes?

10. How might you leverage (diverse perspectives/interdisciplinary collaboration/_____) to enhance your team's innovation?

11. What strategies can you use to integrate (playfulness/curiosity/_____) into your team's daily workflow?

12. How can you remove (hierarchical barriers/fixed mindsets/_____) that inhibit creativity in your team?

13. What methods can you employ to align (team goals/creative pursuits/_____) with the broader vision of the organization?

14. How might you utilize (technology/collaboration tools/_____) to enhance creativity within your team?

15. What steps can you take to build (trust/resilience/_____) among team members to support their creative efforts?

16. How can you foster (critical thinking/lateral thinking/_____) when addressing team challenges?

17. What actions can you take to encourage your team to explore (new trends/emerging technologies/_____) creatively?

18. How might you create a culture of (continuous feedback/iterative improvement/_____) to fuel innovation?

19. What actions can you take to foster (long-term creativity/strategic innovation/_____) while addressing short-term goals?

20. How can you ensure (diversity/inclusion/_____) strengthens the creative outcomes of your team?

21. What steps can you take to develop your team's (emotional intelligence/creative confidence/_____) as part of their growth?

22. How might you adapt your (leadership style/communication approach/_____) to inspire creativity in different personalities?

23. What approaches can you use to transform (setbacks/failures/_____) into opportunities for innovation?

24. How can you nurture (imagination/visionary thinking/_____) in your team's strategic planning sessions?

25. What actions will you take to identify and remove (biases/assumptions/_____) that may hinder creative thinking?

26. How might you empower team members to take ownership of their (creative projects/innovative ideas/_____) for better results?

4. Creative Marketing: Engaging Audiences in New Ways

This chapter explores creative marketing strategies to engage audiences and craft authentic brand stories. These thought-provoking questions are designed to inspire innovative campaigns, connect meaningfully with customers, and differentiate your brand in a competitive marketplace.

1. How can you use (storytelling/emotional engagement/_____) to make your marketing campaigns more impactful?

2. What innovative approaches can you apply to (branding/customer outreach/_____) to captivate your target audience?

3. How might you reframe your (value proposition/brand identity/_____) to stand out in your industry?

4. What (digital tools/social platforms/_____) can you use to create more interactive and engaging marketing content?

5. How can you transform your (product messaging/visual branding/_____) to appeal to a broader audience creatively?

6. What steps can you take to incorporate (user-generated content/audience insights/_____) into your marketing strategy?

7. How could you use (emerging technologies/AI tools/_____) to develop more innovative marketing campaigns?

8. What actions can you take to turn your (customer feedback/market research/_____) into compelling brand stories?

9. How can you leverage (cultural trends/seasonal opportunities/_____) to connect more meaningfully with your audience?

10. What (partnership opportunities/community collaborations/_____) could amplify your marketing reach creatively?

11. How might you infuse (playfulness/curiosity/_____) into your campaigns to surprise and delight your audience?

12. What unconventional strategies could you use to market your (products/services/_____) to a niche audience?

13. How can you reimagine your (brand voice/marketing tone/_____) to better resonate with your ideal customers?

14. What (interactive campaigns/experiential marketing ideas/_____) could you implement to make your brand more memorable?

15. How might you harness (social causes/sustainability efforts/_____) to build a more purpose-driven marketing message?

16. What (visual storytelling techniques/creative formats/_____) could make your marketing content more engaging?

17. How can you rethink your (content strategy/advertising approach/_____) to reflect evolving audience preferences?

18. What actions will you take to explore (new media channels/innovative ad formats/_____) for greater reach?

19. How might you adapt your (email marketing/social media presence/_____) to reflect current market trends creatively?

20. What creative ways can you use (gamification/rewards systems/_____) to increase audience interaction?

21. How can you blend (nostalgia/futuristic themes/_____) into your campaigns to evoke stronger emotional connections?

22. What (personalization techniques/AI-driven insights/_____) can you leverage to tailor your marketing efforts?

23. How could you incorporate (community stories/local perspectives/_____) to add authenticity to your brand narrative?

24. What steps will you take to ensure your (branding strategy/marketing campaigns/_____) align with your business goals innovatively?

25. How can you use (data-driven insights/trend analysis/_____) to anticipate and shape audience expectations?

26. What (creative partnerships/viral strategies/_____) could you explore to boost your brand's visibility effectively?

5. Operations Unleashed: Finding Creativity in Systems and Processes

This chapter explores how creativity can transform business operations, uncovering innovative ways to enhance efficiency and elevate customer satisfaction. These questions are designed to inspire new approaches, streamline processes, and foster operational excellence through imaginative problem-solving.

1. How can you rethink your (workflow design/operational systems/_____) to eliminate inefficiencies?

2. What creative solutions could you explore to optimize your (resource allocation/supply chain/_____)?

3. How might you redesign your (customer service processes/feedback mechanisms/_____) to deliver a better experience?

4. What steps can you take to integrate (automation/AI tools/_____) into your operational strategies?

5. How could you use (data analytics/real-time monitoring/_____) to make your operations more responsive?

6. What innovative approaches can you implement to enhance (team productivity/task management/_____)?

7. How might you leverage (cross-functional collaboration/interdisciplinary input/_____) to address operational challenges?

8. What actions can you take to reduce (waste/time inefficiencies/_____) in your day-to-day processes?

9. How can you improve your (inventory management/logistics/_____) to align better with customer needs?

10. What steps can you take to turn (constraints/operational limitations/_____) into opportunities for innovation?

11. How might you adapt your (standard operating procedures/internal protocols/_____) to reflect evolving business demands?

12. What actions can you take to make your (reporting systems/performance metrics/_____) more dynamic and actionable?

13. How could you foster a culture of (continuous improvement/innovation/_____) within your operations team?

14. What (technologies/tools/_____) could you adopt to enhance efficiency without sacrificing quality?

15. How can you align your (process improvements/operational strategies/_____) with customer expectations?

16. What creative ways can you simplify your (workflows/decision-making processes/_____) to improve outcomes?

17. How might you use (feedback loops/iterative testing/_____) to refine your operational processes?

18. What steps will you take to ensure your (compliance procedures/quality control

standards/_____) remain adaptable and innovative?

19. How could you redesign your (employee training/onboarding programs/_____) to make them more impactful?

20. What creative approaches can you apply to reduce (costs/errors/_____) without compromising efficiency?

21. How might you transform your (customer fulfillment/delivery systems/_____) to exceed expectations?

22. What (collaborations/external partnerships/_____) could you explore to strengthen your operational processes?

23. How can you incorporate (sustainability practices/green initiatives/_____) into your daily operations creatively?

24. What role can (predictive analytics/forecasting tools/_____) play in improving your operational planning?

25. How might you encourage your team to think creatively about (problem-solving/process improvements/_____) in their roles?

26. What innovative methods can you implement to turn (customer complaints/operational setbacks/_____) into actionable insights?

6. Turning Data into Inspiration: Creativity in Analytics

This chapter helps you transform data into actionable insights that drive creativity and innovation. These questions encourage you to explore unique ways of interpreting data, uncovering opportunities, and applying analytics to inspire forward-thinking decisions and strategies.

1. How can you use (data patterns/trend analysis/_____) to identify new opportunities in your business?

2. What creative approaches can you apply to visualize your (key metrics/customer insights/_____) for better understanding?

3. How might you transform (raw data/historical reports/_____) into actionable strategies for the future?

4. What role can (predictive analytics/AI tools/_____) play in reimagining your business processes?

5. How could you combine (quantitative data/qualitative feedback/_____) to generate unique insights?

6. What steps can you take to uncover (hidden trends/untapped potential/_____) in your data?

7. How might you reframe your (data interpretation/dashboard designs/_____) to spark innovative ideas?

8. What (visualization techniques/data storytelling methods/_____) can you use to make complex data more engaging?

9. How can you encourage your team to use (data-driven insights/analytics tools/_____) creatively in decision-making?

10. What innovative ways could you analyze your (customer behavior patterns/sales trends/_____) to find unexpected connections?

11. How might you repurpose (existing datasets/internal reports/_____) to address emerging challenges?

12. What steps can you take to transform your (business intelligence reports/operational data/_____) into inspiration for new strategies?

13. How could you creatively use (real-time analytics/streaming data/_____) to adapt to shifting market demands?

14. What methods can you apply to integrate (external data sources/competitor insights/_____) into your strategy creatively?

15. How can you align your (data goals/analytics KPIs/_____) with your long-term innovation strategy?

16. What (technologies/automation tools/_____) could you adopt to make your data analysis more dynamic?

17. How might you reinterpret your (financial data/marketing metrics/_____) to uncover growth opportunities?

18. What steps can you take to make your (data dashboards/reports/_____) more intuitive and inspiring for your team?

19. How can you leverage (machine learning/advanced modeling/_____) to turn data into actionable foresight?

20. What creative ways can you use (historical trends/seasonal data/_____) to anticipate future customer needs?

21. How might you improve your (collaboration processes/team discussions/_____) to explore the full potential of your analytics?

22. What (unexpected variables/external factors/_____) could you explore in your data to uncover unique insights?

23. How can you ensure that your (data strategy/analytics approach/_____) remains adaptive and forward-thinking?

24. What (storytelling methods/communication strategies/_____) could you use to inspire others with your data insights?

25. How could you integrate (real-world context/customer stories/_____) into your data interpretation to add depth and creativity?

26. What steps will you take to foster a culture of (exploration/innovation/_____) in how your team interacts with data?

7. Problem Solving as an Art: Overcoming Business Challenges

This chapter encourages you to view problem-solving as a creative art. These questions are designed to help you reframe challenges, explore unconventional solutions, and navigate roadblocks with innovation, fostering resilience and adaptability in business situations.

1. What actions will you take to address your (current roadblocks/recurring challenges/_____) using fresh perspectives?

2. How can you reframe your (business problems/operational bottlenecks/_____) to uncover hidden opportunities?

3. What (brainstorming techniques/creative frameworks/_____) can you use to approach your biggest challenge differently?

4. How might you collaborate with (cross-functional teams/external experts/_____) to solve persistent issues?

5. What role can (empathy/active listening/_____) play in uncovering the root cause of a problem?

6. How could you turn (constraints/resource limitations/_____) into advantages for innovative solutions?

7. What actions will you take to test (unconventional ideas/out-of-the-box solutions/_____) for a persistent challenge?

8. How can you use (scenario planning/reverse engineering/_____) to rethink a difficult situation?

9. What creative strategies can you apply to resolve (conflicts/communication breakdowns/_____) within your team?

10. How might you use (visualization techniques/mind mapping/_____) to gain clarity on complex problems?

11. What steps can you take to transform (failures/setbacks/_____) into lessons for creative growth?

12. How could you adapt (successful strategies/past experiences/_____) to address your current challenges?

13. What role can (prototyping/rapid experimentation/_____) play in testing potential solutions?

14. How might you use (feedback loops/iterative improvements/_____) to refine your approach to a problem?

15. What (emerging technologies/new tools/_____) can you explore to tackle recurring obstacles creatively?

16. How can you use (customer feedback/market insights/_____) to rethink your approach to a business challenge?

17. What creative ways can you employ to simplify your (decision-making/problem-solving process/_____)?

18. How might you approach your (crisis management strategies/team interventions/_____) from a fresh angle?

19. What steps can you take to foster a (problem-solving culture/innovative mindset/_____) within your team?

20. How could you apply (lateral thinking/design thinking/_____) to resolve a critical issue?

21. What actions can you take to break down (complex challenges/overwhelming problems/_____) into smaller, manageable pieces?

22. How might you incorporate (playful techniques/gamification/_____) to approach problem-solving creatively?

23. What steps will you take to turn (ambiguity/uncertainty/_____) into a space for innovation and opportunity?

24. How can you use (data insights/real-time feedback/_____) to make informed decisions during crises?

25. What (collaborative opportunities/external perspectives/_____) could you leverage to uncover unique solutions?

26. How might you cultivate (resilience/creative confidence/_____) to navigate future challenges more effectively?

8. Building Collaborative Creativity: Harnessing Group Genius

This chapter focuses on unleashing the creative power of teams by fostering collaboration and synergy. These questions are designed to inspire leaders and teams to think collectively, solve problems innovatively, and build environments that encourage shared creativity.

1. How can you create opportunities for your team to share (bold ideas/unconventional solutions/_____) more openly?

2. What actions can you take to encourage (cross-departmental collaboration/interdisciplinary teamwork/_____) within your organization?

3. How might you foster (trust/open communication/_____) to unlock your team's collective creativity?

4. What (collaborative tools/team activities/_____) could you use to enhance group brainstorming sessions?

5. How can you balance (individual contributions/group dynamics/_____) to achieve creative synergy?

6. What steps can you take to ensure your team feels (valued/empowered/_____) to voice innovative ideas?

7. How could you use (shared goals/vision alignment/_____) to inspire creativity across different team roles?

8. What actions will you take to remove (hierarchical barriers/siloed thinking/_____) that hinder collaborative innovation?

9. How can you leverage (diverse perspectives/different skill sets/_____) to improve group problem-solving?

10. What steps might you take to cultivate a (safe space/supportive culture/_____) for experimental thinking in your team?

11. How could you introduce (playful elements/gamified approaches/_____) to make collaboration more engaging and creative?

12. What (team rituals/collaborative processes/_____) can you establish to sustain a culture of collective creativity?

13. How might you encourage your team to approach (feedback sessions/project reviews/_____) as opportunities for collaborative growth?

14. What actions can you take to integrate (remote team members/cross-border collaborations/_____) into creative discussions seamlessly?

15. How can you use (technology platforms/shared digital spaces/_____) to enhance real-time collaboration?

16. What strategies might you employ to resolve (creative conflicts/disagreements/_____) in a constructive way?

17. How can you motivate your team to co-create (innovative solutions/future strategies/_____) for current challenges?

18. What role can (diversity and inclusion/shared leadership/_____) play in strengthening collaborative innovation?

19. How might you adapt your (meeting formats/brainstorming sessions/_____) to maximize team creativity?

20. What (external partnerships/guest contributors/_____) could you introduce to inspire new thinking in your group?

21. How can you recognize and celebrate (team milestones/shared achievements/_____) to encourage ongoing collaboration?

22. What steps will you take to align your team's (creative processes/decision-making approaches/_____) with organizational objectives?

23. How could you use (feedback loops/iterative collaboration/_____) to refine and elevate group projects?

24. What creative exercises can you implement to strengthen your team's (communication/problem-solving abilities/_____) together?

25. How can you encourage your team to embrace (ambiguity/uncertainty/_____) as a space for collective innovation?

26. What actions will you take to foster a culture of (collaborative learning/shared experimentation/_____) in your organization?

9. Disrupt Yourself: Personal Creativity for Professional Growth

This chapter invites you to disrupt your habits and unleash your personal creativity for professional growth. These questions are designed to help you break routines, challenge assumptions, and discover new ways to innovate and grow personally and professionally.

1. What actions will you take to step outside your (comfort zone/established routines/_____) this week?

2. How might you challenge your (daily habits/automatic behaviors/_____) to discover fresh perspectives?

3. What steps can you take to explore (new interests/unfamiliar environments/_____) that inspire your creativity?

4. How can you reframe your (goals/personal challenges/_____) to encourage innovative solutions?

5. What (skills/mindsets/_____) could you learn or strengthen to enhance your creative thinking?

6. How might you turn (past failures/lessons learned/_____) into opportunities for creative growth?

7. What actions can you take to disrupt your (thought patterns/problem-solving approaches/_____) and foster innovation?

8. How can you use (journaling/self-reflection/_____) to uncover untapped creative potential?

9. What (books/resources/_____) could you explore to spark new ideas and insights?

10. How might you use (playful experimentation/mindfulness/_____) to reinvigorate your creative thinking?

11. What role can (collaboration/mentorship/_____) play in helping you expand your creative boundaries?

12. How can you reimagine your (workspace/personal environment/_____) to inspire innovation?

13. What creative risks are you willing to take in your (career/personal projects/_____) to achieve breakthrough results?

14. How might you approach your (daily challenges/recurring problems/_____) from a completely new angle?

15. What (unexpected hobbies/creative outlets/_____) could you pursue to expand your imagination?

16. How can you shift your (self-perception/personal narrative/_____) to build creative confidence?

17. What steps might you take to integrate (diverse perspectives/new collaborations/_____) into your personal growth journey?

18. How could you use (time-blocking/unstructured thinking time/_____) to prioritize creative exploration?

19. What actions will you take to confront and overcome (self-doubt/fear of failure/_____) in your creative pursuits?

20. How can you incorporate (technology/tools/_____) to amplify your personal creativity?

21. What habits can you replace with (intentional reflection/deliberate practice/_____) to spark innovation in your daily life?

22. How might you use (feedback from others/self-assessments/_____) to refine and elevate your creative process?

23. What steps will you take to cultivate a mindset of (curiosity/continuous learning/_____) in your personal growth?

24. How can you approach (ambiguity/uncertainty/_____) as a source of creative opportunity rather than a barrier?

25. What (visions/long-term aspirations/_____) inspire you to embrace change and foster personal creativity?

26. How might you celebrate your (small wins/daily progress/_____) to sustain momentum in your creative journey?

10. The Future of Work: Preparing for Emerging Opportunities

This chapter explores how creativity will shape the future of work, industries, and technologies. These questions are designed to help professionals anticipate emerging opportunities, adapt to change, and develop innovative strategies for thriving in tomorrow's dynamic business landscape.

1. What steps will you take to integrate (emerging technologies/automation tools/_____) into your workflow creatively?

2. How might you reimagine your (business model/operational strategies/_____) to align with future trends?

3. What actions can you take to prepare for the impact of (AI-driven insights/remote collaboration tools/_____) on your industry?

4. How can you anticipate changes in (customer expectations/market dynamics/_____) and innovate to stay ahead?

5. What creative approaches can you use to rethink your (talent acquisition/workforce planning/_____) in the age of automation?

6. How might you leverage (sustainability principles/green technologies/_____) to address future business challenges?

7. What steps will you take to ensure your (company culture/team collaboration/_____) remains adaptable in a fast-changing environment?

8. How could you use (scenario planning/futuristic simulations/_____) to prepare for disruptive shifts in your industry?

9. What role can (upskilling/continuous learning/_____) play in preparing you and your team for the future of work?

10. How can you embrace (diversity/inclusion/_____) as a creative advantage in shaping future strategies?

11. What steps might you take to align your (technology investments/innovation goals/_____) with long-term opportunities?

12. How could you use (data analytics/trend forecasting/_____) to identify untapped potential in your market?

13. What creative ways can you prepare for changes in (workforce expectations/workplace flexibility/_____)?

14. How might you approach (ethical decision-making/sustainability practices/_____) to thrive in an increasingly conscious marketplace?

15. What (cross-industry partnerships/global collaborations/_____) could you explore to drive innovation for future needs?

16. How can you redesign your (work environment/employee experience/_____) to encourage creativity in the workplace of the future?

17. What steps will you take to use (artificial intelligence/machine learning/_____) as a catalyst for innovation in your field?

18. How might you turn (technological disruption/market uncertainty/_____) into opportunities for growth and innovation?

19. What creative strategies could you implement to navigate the (gig economy/flexible work structures/_____) more effectively?

20. How can you anticipate and address shifts in (global supply chains/consumer behavior/_____) creatively?

21. What actions can you take to align your (leadership style/organizational goals/_____) with the future demands of work?

22. How might you adapt your (business strategies/workforce training/_____) to reflect emerging industry standards?

23. What role can (innovation hubs/digital platforms/_____) play in preparing your organization for the future?

24. How can you foster a mindset of (adaptability/forward-thinking/_____) within your team to embrace change?

25. What creative tools can you use to bridge the gap between (human creativity/technological capabilities/_____)?

26. How might you redefine your (long-term vision/core values/_____) to stay relevant and innovative in the years ahead?

11. Creative Ethics: Balancing Innovation with Responsibility

This chapter emphasizes the importance of balancing innovation with responsibility. These questions are designed to inspire professionals to align creativity with ethical practices, ensuring sustainable, socially responsible solutions while driving innovation and positive impact in their industries.

1. How can you align your (creative processes/innovation goals/_____) with ethical principles to ensure long-term impact?

2. What steps can you take to incorporate (sustainability/social responsibility/_____) into your business innovations?

3. How might you evaluate the (ethical implications/social effects/_____) of a new idea or product?

4. What role can (transparency/accountability/_____) play in ensuring your creative efforts remain ethical?

5. How can you use (stakeholder input/community feedback/_____) to guide your ethical decision-making in innovation?

6. What creative approaches can you explore to balance (profitability/social good/_____) in your business model?

7. How might you address (potential biases/unintended consequences/_____) in your creative process?

8. What actions can you take to make your (supply chain/product lifecycle/_____) more sustainable?

9. How can you reframe your (mission/organizational goals/_____) to reflect a stronger commitment to ethical innovation?

10. What steps will you take to ensure your (marketing practices/customer engagement/_____) align with ethical standards?

11. How might you use (regulations/industry guidelines/_____) as a foundation for ethical creativity?

12. What (ethical dilemmas/social challenges/_____) do you foresee in your field, and how can creativity address them?

13. How could you balance the needs of (current stakeholders/future generations/_____) in your innovation strategies?

14. What (collaborations/community partnerships/_____) can you pursue to strengthen the social impact of your ideas?

15. How can you turn (limitations/resource constraints/_____) into opportunities for sustainable innovation?

16. What actions can you take to improve (diversity/equity/_____) in your creative processes?

17. How might you adapt your (leadership style/team culture/_____) to prioritize ethical practices in innovation?

18. What role can (education/awareness campaigns/_____) play in embedding ethics into your creative strategies?

19. How can you assess the (long-term consequences/environmental impact/_____) of your innovative ideas?

20. What creative ways can you ensure your (digital tools/technological innovations/_____) respect privacy and promote fairness?

21. How might you address (cultural differences/social sensitivities/_____) in your creative work to make it inclusive?

22. What actions will you take to ensure your (intellectual property/product designs/_____) do not exploit vulnerable communities?

23. How can you build a framework for (ethical risk assessment/social impact evaluation/_____) in your organization?

24. What steps can you take to foster (open dialogue/shared values/_____) about ethics in your creative teams?

25. How might you turn (ethical challenges/social concerns/_____) into catalysts for innovative solutions?

26. What creative methods can you use to communicate your (ethical values/corporate responsibility/_____) to your audience effectively?

12. Putting It All Together: A Blueprint for Creative Action

This chapter focuses on translating creativity into tangible results by synthesizing lessons into actionable frameworks. These questions help professionals build personalized plans, integrate creative strategies into their goals, and take purposeful steps to achieve meaningful innovation.

1. What actions will you take this week to apply your (creative insights/new ideas/_____) to your current projects?

2. How can you integrate your (big-picture goals/actionable steps/_____) into a cohesive plan for success?

3. What specific steps will you take to turn your (innovative concepts/brainstorming ideas/_____) into actionable outcomes?

4. How can you use your (strengths/past successes/_____) to create a roadmap for implementing creativity?

5. What methods can you employ to balance (short-term goals/long-term aspirations/_____) in your creative blueprint?

6. How might you prioritize (key actions/impactful ideas/_____) to maximize the effectiveness of your plan?

7. What tools will you use to track progress on your (creative initiatives/personal milestones/_____)?

8. How can you align your (team objectives/individual goals/_____) with your creative strategy?

9. What (metrics/indicators/_____) will you define to measure the success of your creative plan?

10. How might you adapt your (frameworks/workflows/_____) to incorporate continuous innovation?

11. What actions will you take to overcome (roadblocks/resistance/_____) that may arise during execution?

12. How can you use (feedback loops/iterative processes/_____) to refine and improve your creative plan?

13. What steps will you take to ensure that your (action plan/team contributions/_____) stay aligned with your core vision?

14. How might you use (collaboration/external partnerships/_____) to enhance the effectiveness of your blueprint?

15. What strategies will you implement to ensure (consistency/flexibility/_____) in achieving your creative goals?

16. How can you transform your (vision/ideas/_____) into specific, measurable, and actionable objectives?

17. What creative approaches can you apply to break down (complex challenges/overwhelming tasks/_____) into manageable steps?

18. How might you incorporate (data-driven insights/personal intuition/_____) to guide your creative actions?

19. What actions will you take to ensure your (daily habits/work routines/_____) support your overall creative plan?

20. How can you leverage (technology/resources/_____) to streamline the implementation of your strategy?

21. What role can (mentors/team members/_____) play in holding you accountable for executing your plan?

22. How might you use (visualization techniques/checklists/_____) to stay focused on your creative goals?

23. What (small wins/early successes/_____) can you celebrate to build momentum as you implement your creative framework?

24. How can you align your (learning goals/future aspirations/_____) with your current creative priorities?

25. What actions will you take to maintain (adaptability/resilience/_____) as you execute and refine your plan?

26. How can you ensure that your (creative strategies/final blueprint/_____) remain relevant and impactful in the future?

13. Closing Reflections: The Lifelong Creative Journey

This chapter encourages readers to view creativity as a lifelong journey. These reflective questions are designed to inspire ongoing innovation, personal growth, and a deep commitment to embracing creativity as an essential part of professional and personal development.

1. What actions will you take to nurture your (creative mindset/personal growth/_____) on an ongoing basis?

2. How can you integrate (daily habits/lifelong learning/_____) to sustain your creative journey?

3. What steps will you take to revisit and refine your (creative goals/long-term vision/_____) regularly?

4. How might you use (past experiences/lessons learned/_____) to fuel your ongoing creative evolution?

5. What (new skills/different perspectives/_____) will you explore to keep your creativity fresh and dynamic?

6. How can you use (self-reflection/feedback from others/_____) to identify opportunities for creative improvement?

7. What specific actions will you take to build a (support network/community of innovators/_____) that inspires your creativity?

8. How might you balance (innovation/consistency/_____) as part of your lifelong creative process?

9. What (moments of success/challenges overcome/_____) can you celebrate as milestones in your creative journey?

10. How will you ensure your (values/personal mission/_____) remain central to your creative practice?

11. What actions can you take to explore (emerging trends/new disciplines/_____) that inspire innovation?

12. How can you reframe (setbacks/failures/_____) as essential steps in your creative growth?

13. What role can (mentorship/shared experiences/_____) play in deepening your creativity over time?

14. How might you develop a (personal ritual/structured reflection/_____) to stay connected to your creative purpose?

15. What (books/resources/_____) will you seek out to challenge and expand your creative thinking?

16. How can you ensure that your (creative energy/focus/_____) remains aligned with your evolving goals?

17. What (memories/experiences/_____) have shaped your creativity, and how might they guide your future efforts?

18. How can you transform your (daily routine/long-term practices/_____) to continuously spark inspiration?

19. What actions will you take to embrace (uncertainty/change/_____) as part of your creative growth?

20. How might you share your (creative insights/innovative ideas/_____) with others to inspire and motivate them?

21. What steps will you take to reflect on your (accomplishments/creative impact/_____) regularly?

22. How can you approach (new challenges/opportunities/_____) as catalysts for ongoing innovation?

23. What (small wins/daily breakthroughs/_____) will you celebrate to stay motivated in your creative journey?

24. How might you adapt your (creative practices/innovation strategies/_____) to stay relevant in a changing world?

25. What role can (gratitude/self-compassion/_____) play in sustaining your creative momentum over the long term?

26. How will you ensure your (creative passion/innovative mindset/_____) continues to thrive as you grow personally and professionally?

14. Operational Efficiency as a Creativity Challenge

This chapter explores operational efficiency as a creative challenge, focusing on optimizing workflows, reducing waste, and designing customer-centric systems. These questions inspire innovative approaches to enhance processes, embrace lean practices, and turn constraints into opportunities for success.

1. How can you use (data insights/customer feedback/_____) to identify inefficiencies in your current workflows?

2. What creative approaches can you explore to simplify your (processes/decision-making systems/_____) without sacrificing quality?

3. How might you integrate (lean principles/Six Sigma practices/_____) with creativity to improve operations?

4. What (innovative tools/automation strategies/_____) could you adopt to reduce waste in your operations?

5. How can you reframe your (resource constraints/operational bottlenecks/_____) as opportunities for innovative solutions?

6. What steps will you take to redesign your (customer journey/supply chain/_____) to make it more efficient and customer-focused?

7. How might you encourage your team to think creatively about (problem-solving/workflow optimization/_____) in their daily roles?

8. What (collaborative efforts/team brainstorming sessions/_____) could uncover fresh ideas for improving operational efficiency?

9. How can you use (real-time data/predictive analytics/_____) to proactively address operational challenges?

10. What role can (customer insights/market trends/_____) play in shaping your operational strategies?

11. How might you rethink your (inventory management/resource allocation/_____) to better align with lean innovation principles?

12. What (small changes/micro-innovations/_____) could you implement to create a more agile operational system?

13. How can you incorporate (sustainability practices/green innovations/_____) into your operations to reduce waste and costs?

14. What creative ways can you approach (process mapping/workflow analysis/_____) to uncover inefficiencies?

15. How might you transform your (employee feedback/customer complaints/_____) into actionable improvements for operational efficiency?

16. What actions can you take to balance (speed/quality/_____) in delivering operational excellence?

17. How can you use (cross-functional teams/external partnerships/_____) to bring new perspectives to process improvement?

18. What steps will you take to optimize your (equipment utilization/resource scheduling/_____) for better performance?

19. How might you apply (design thinking/agile methodologies/_____) to rethink traditional operational processes?

20. What creative approaches could you use to ensure your (quality assurance/standard operating procedures/_____) remain adaptive and innovative?

21. How can you redesign your (training programs/employee onboarding/_____) to empower employees in driving operational efficiency?

22. What (unconventional ideas/breakthrough technologies/_____) could revolutionize your approach to operational workflows?

23. How might you encourage (continuous improvement/cultural innovation/_____) within your team to sustain operational success?

24. What steps will you take to integrate (customer-centric metrics/performance dashboards/_____) for better decision-making?

25. How can you use (lessons from other industries/case studies/_____) to inspire creative solutions for your operational challenges?

26. What actions will you take to ensure your (process improvements/workflow designs/_____) adapt to future business needs?

15. Financial Creativity: Innovative Approaches to Managing Resources

This chapter explores innovative financial strategies to optimize resources, fuel growth, and adapt to competitive markets. These questions encourage creative approaches to funding, budgeting, pricing, and cost management, helping businesses achieve efficiency and maximize value without compromising quality.

1. What steps can you take to explore (alternative funding sources/venture capital hybrids/_____) to support your growth initiatives?

2. How might you redesign your (budgeting process/resource allocation/_____) to maximize ROI creatively?

3. What innovative approaches could you apply to reduce (operational costs/overhead expenses/_____) without sacrificing quality?

4. How can you leverage (crowdfunding/digital platforms/_____) to finance new projects or initiatives?

5. What creative strategies could you use to adjust your (pricing models/revenue streams/_____) in competitive markets?

6. How might you align your (financial goals/budgeting priorities/_____) with long-term innovation objectives?

7. What (partnership opportunities/collaborative ventures/_____) could help you pool resources and lower financial risks?

8. How can you use (financial data/forecasting tools/_____) to uncover hidden opportunities for savings or growth?

9. What actions will you take to optimize your (inventory management/cash flow/_____) for financial stability?

10. How might you apply (agile principles/lean methodologies/_____) to enhance your financial efficiency?

11. What role can (subscription models/performance-based pricing/_____) play in reshaping your revenue structure?

12. How can you approach (negotiations/supplier agreements/_____) more creatively to reduce costs or gain value?

13. What steps will you take to introduce (tiered pricing/innovative discounts/_____) to attract and retain customers?

14. How might you rethink your (funding pitch/financial presentation/_____) to appeal to nontraditional investors?

15. What actions can you take to repurpose (existing assets/excess inventory/_____) for greater financial returns?

16. How might you use (shared services/outsourcing/_____) to achieve operational cost savings?

17. What creative methods could you implement to improve (profit margins/resource utilization/_____) across departments?

18. How can you incentivize (customer loyalty/repeat purchases/_____) through innovative pricing strategies?

19. What steps will you take to ensure your (financial plans/cost-saving initiatives/_____) align with your company's mission?

20. How can you integrate (sustainability goals/green investments/_____) into your financial strategy for long-term value?

21. What (digital tools/automated systems/_____) can you adopt to streamline financial processes and reduce manual errors?

22. How might you approach (risk management/investment diversification/_____) to ensure sustainable growth?

23. What actions can you take to create (flexible budgets/contingency funds/_____) that adapt to changing market conditions?

24. How can you balance (short-term financial needs/long-term investments/_____) to ensure sustainable innovation?

25. What creative solutions might you explore to turn (economic downturns/resource constraints/_____) into opportunities for growth?

26. How can you measure the success of your (financial experiments/new pricing models/_____) to continuously refine your approach?

16. Creative Negotiation and Relationship Management

This chapter emphasizes creativity as a vital tool in negotiation and relationship management. These questions inspire professionals to think innovatively about building trust, fostering win-win outcomes, and leveraging technology to enhance partnerships, stakeholder management, and customer relationships.

1. How can you use (active listening/empathy/_____) to build trust during negotiations?

2. What creative strategies can you apply to turn (conflicts/differences/_____) into win-win outcomes?

3. How might you reframe your (approach to objections/negotiation tactics/_____) to achieve a better resolution?

4. What actions can you take to incorporate (non-verbal cues/behavioral insights/_____) into your negotiation style?

5. How can you use (digital tools/AI-driven insights/_____) to enhance your customer relationship management?

6. What role can (collaborative brainstorming/idea-sharing sessions/_____) play in strengthening partnerships?

7. How might you adapt your (negotiation tone/relationship-building strategies/_____) to suit diverse stakeholders?

8. What creative methods could you implement to resolve (stakeholder disputes/communication breakdowns/_____) effectively?

9. How can you leverage (mutual goals/shared incentives/_____) to align with your negotiation counterpart?

10. What (new technologies/innovative CRM tools/_____) could help you manage relationships more effectively?

11. How might you turn (shared challenges/mutual risks/_____) into opportunities for collaboration?

12. What steps can you take to use (feedback loops/ongoing communication/_____) to strengthen stakeholder trust?

13. How can you design a (customized proposal/unique value offer/_____) that appeals to your partner's priorities?

14. What (cultural insights/personalized approaches/_____) could you use to enhance your relationships with international clients?

15. How might you use (storytelling/narrative techniques/_____) to make your pitch more persuasive?

16. What creative approaches can you apply to maintain (long-term partnerships/ongoing client relationships/_____) effectively?

17. How can you turn (rejection/setbacks/_____) into learning opportunities for future negotiations?

18. What (metrics/relationship benchmarks/_____) can you develop to measure the success of your stakeholder management efforts?

19. How might you adapt your (collaborative strategies/conflict resolution skills/_____) to dynamic relationship needs?

20. What role can (sustainability initiatives/social responsibility/_____) play in enhancing your negotiation approach?

21. How can you creatively involve (third-party mediators/cross-functional teams/_____) to facilitate challenging negotiations?

22. What actions will you take to address (power imbalances/stakeholder demands/_____) in a creative and ethical way?

23. How might you use (gamification/interactive tools/_____) to engage stakeholders in relationship-building processes?

24. What steps can you take to turn (complex contracts/multifaceted agreements/_____) into simplified, mutually beneficial solutions?

25. How can you align your (brand values/business mission/_____) with relationship-building strategies to create stronger connections?

26. What creative approaches might you explore to ensure your (negotiation results/relationship outcomes/_____) are sustainable in the long term?

17. Customer Experience Innovation: Creating Memorable Interactions

This chapter explores innovative approaches to creating exceptional customer experiences. By focusing on human-centered design, personalization, and leveraging AI, these questions inspire professionals to redefine how businesses deliver value and forge memorable connections with their customers.

1. How can you use (customer feedback/data insights/_____) to redesign your customer journey creatively?

2. What actions will you take to personalize your (interactions/service offerings/_____) at scale without losing a human touch?

3. How might you use (AI-driven tools/predictive analytics/_____) to anticipate and exceed customer needs?

4. What (touchpoints/critical moments/_____) in your customer journey could you redesign for greater impact?

5. How can you integrate (human-centered design/innovative storytelling/_____) into crafting memorable customer experiences?

6. What role can (empathy/active listening/_____) play in transforming your approach to customer service?

7. How might you use (loyalty programs/personalized rewards/_____) to deepen customer engagement?

8. What creative ways can you address (customer pain points/reoccurring challenges/_____) to enhance satisfaction?

9. How can you apply (real-time data/customer behavior tracking/_____) to improve service responsiveness?

10. What steps will you take to turn your (brand values/mission statement/_____) into tangible customer experiences?

11. How might you design (immersive experiences/interactive platforms/_____) that captivate your customers?

12. What creative methods can you use to ensure (consistency/uniqueness/_____) across all customer touchpoints?

13. How can you leverage (cross-functional teams/external collaborations/_____) to innovate in customer experience design?

14. What (unexpected elements/playful surprises/_____) could you incorporate to delight your customers?

15. How might you adapt your (service delivery/communication channels/_____) to reflect evolving customer expectations?

16. What role can (visual storytelling/brand narratives/_____) play in building stronger emotional connections with your customers?

17. How can you creatively use (social media/online communities/_____) to enhance your customer experience strategy?

18. What actions will you take to turn (complaints/negative feedback/_____) into opportunities for creating better experiences?

19. How might you utilize (VR/AR technologies/_____) to deliver cutting-edge customer interactions?

20. What (inclusive practices/cultural sensitivities/_____) can you implement to ensure your experiences resonate globally?

21. How can you innovate your (customer onboarding/first impression touchpoints/_____) to set a high standard from the start?

22. What creative approaches can you apply to align your (team training/customer-focused initiatives/_____) with experience goals?

23. How might you use (data visualizations/user-friendly dashboards/_____) to empower your customers with meaningful insights?

24. What steps can you take to balance (automation/personalization/_____) in your customer experience design?

25. How could you reimagine your (feedback systems/survey methods/_____) to make them engaging and actionable?

26. What creative strategies can you implement to turn your (brand promises/customer interactions/_____) into lasting impressions?

18. Crisis Creativity: Thriving Under Pressure

This chapter focuses on harnessing creativity to thrive during crises and uncertainty. These questions inspire innovative strategies, adaptability, and effective communication, helping businesses navigate challenges while identifying opportunities for growth and transformation under pressure.

1. What steps can you take to turn (current challenges/operational constraints/_____) into opportunities for innovation?

2. How can you use (team collaboration/customer feedback/_____) to develop creative solutions during crises?

3. What role can (flexibility/rapid prototyping/_____) play in helping your business adapt to uncertain circumstances?

4. How might you reimagine your (product offerings/service delivery/_____) to better meet customer needs during a crisis?

5. What (emerging trends/technological advancements/_____) could you leverage to stay ahead during uncertain times?

6. How can you redefine your (communication strategies/messaging/_____) to connect authentically with your stakeholders during adversity?

7. What actions will you take to encourage (innovative thinking/problem-solving/_____) across your team during high-pressure situations?

8. How might you use (past setbacks/lessons learned/_____) to inform your approach to current challenges?

9. What creative approaches can you apply to balance (short-term survival/long-term goals/_____) during a crisis?

10. How can you foster (resilience/adaptability/_____) within your team to navigate uncertainty more effectively?

11. What (new partnerships/external collaborations/_____) could help you address resource gaps during a crisis?

12. How might you adapt your (marketing strategy/brand messaging/_____) to align with shifting customer priorities?

13. What steps can you take to streamline your (operations/decision-making processes/_____) for agility during crises?

14. How can you use (scenario planning/future simulations/_____) to prepare for potential disruptions?

15. What creative methods could you implement to maintain (employee morale/customer trust/_____) during challenging periods?

16. How might you transform (limited budgets/resource shortages/_____) into creative strengths for innovation?

17. What actions will you take to ensure your (core values/brand purpose/_____) remain intact while adapting to new realities?

18. How can you use (data insights/real-time feedback/_____) to make swift and effective decisions during a crisis?

19. What role can (digital tools/automation/_____) play in helping your business stay operational during disruption?

20. How might you turn (unexpected disruptions/market volatility/_____) into new growth opportunities?

21. What steps can you take to build (stronger contingency plans/creative response frameworks/_____) for future crises?

22. How can you innovate your (supply chain/logistics/_____) to remain resilient during unexpected challenges?

23. What (alternative revenue streams/creative business models/_____) could you explore to sustain your business during downturns?

24. How might you empower your team to embrace (risk-taking/experimental thinking/_____) during high-pressure situations?

25. What (case studies/inspirational examples/_____) can you draw from to guide your creative approach to crisis management?

26. How can you ensure your (communication/transparency/_____) builds trust and aligns with stakeholder needs during a crisis?

19. Cross-Industry Creativity: Learning from Unexpected Sources

This chapter explores how insights from diverse industries can spark innovation in your business. These questions encourage professionals to look beyond traditional competitors, draw inspiration from unexpected sources, and adapt creative strategies from other sectors to their own challenges.

1. What actions can you take to explore (innovations/trends/_____) in unrelated industries for ideas that could transform your business?

2. How might you adapt (gamification/customer engagement strategies/_____) from other sectors to improve your offerings?

3. What lessons can you draw from (healthcare/logistics/_____) to address challenges in your industry?

4. How can you benchmark your (customer service/product design/_____) against companies in vastly different fields?

5. What role can (collaborations with unconventional partners/inspiration trips/_____) play in bringing fresh ideas to your business?

6. How might you apply (subscription models/personalization techniques/_____) from other industries to create new revenue streams?

7. What steps can you take to integrate (sustainability innovations/digital tools/_____) from unrelated fields into your operations?

8. How can you use (cross-industry comparisons/case studies/_____) to rethink your approach to problem-solving?

9. What (processes/tools/_____) from industries like aviation or hospitality could improve your operational efficiency?

10. How might you incorporate (design thinking/experience-driven approaches/_____) from other industries into your strategy?

11. What actions will you take to learn from (startups/large-scale enterprises/_____) in fields unrelated to your own?

12. How can you creatively reframe your (business challenges/goals/_____) by viewing them through the lens of another sector?

13. What (cultural practices/global trends/_____) from other industries could inspire innovation in your business?

14. How might you adapt (automation techniques/AI applications/_____) from tech-heavy industries to simplify your processes?

15. What role can (customer journey mapping/behavioral insights/_____) from other sectors play in improving your customer experience?

16. How can you use (supply chain innovations/resource-sharing practices/_____) from different industries to reduce costs and waste?

17. What (event management/community engagement practices/_____) could you borrow

from industries known for large-scale coordination?

18. How might you introduce (creative pricing models/loyalty programs/_____) inspired by industries like gaming or retail?

19. What (technology trends/data visualization tools/_____) from unrelated fields can you leverage for strategic decisions?

20. How can you use (branding strategies/advertising techniques/_____) from creative industries to strengthen your brand?

21. What (collaborative exercises/networking practices/_____) from other industries can help your team think outside the box?

22. How might you adopt (product development methods/service protocols/_____) from healthcare, education, or entertainment industries?

23. What actions can you take to study (cross-industry mergers/partnerships/_____) and apply their principles to your growth strategy?

24. How can you translate (logistics systems/workflow structures/_____) from industries like shipping or manufacturing into your operations?

25. What steps will you take to adapt (customer-centric innovations/team management practices/_____) from other fields into your organization?

26. How might you use (trendspotting methods/competitor analysis/_____) across

industries to stay ahead of the curve in your market?

20. Sustainability and Purpose-Driven Creativity

This chapter explores how businesses can align creativity with sustainability and social impact. These questions are designed to inspire innovative strategies that incorporate ethical practices, environmental stewardship, and purpose-driven models to achieve lasting value for businesses and society.

1. What steps can you take to design (products/services/_____) that align with circular economy principles?

2. How might you reduce (waste/environmental impact/_____) in your processes without compromising quality or efficiency?

3. What role can (renewable resources/sustainable materials/_____) play in your creative projects or product designs?

4. How can you align your (business goals/innovation strategies/_____) with sustainability objectives?

5. What creative approaches could you use to address (supply chain emissions/resource inefficiencies/_____) in your operations?

6. How might you turn (customer feedback/market demand/_____) for sustainable solutions into a competitive advantage?

7. What actions will you take to integrate (ethics/social impact/_____) into your product development lifecycle?

8. How can you use (recycling initiatives/resource-sharing systems/_____) to improve your company's sustainability efforts?

9. What (collaborations/external partnerships/_____) could you explore to enhance your sustainability and purpose-driven goals?

10. How might you use (technology/data analytics/_____) to track and improve your environmental footprint?

11. What creative methods can you implement to make your (branding/marketing/_____) reflect your commitment to sustainability?

12. How can you redesign your (packaging/logistics/_____) to minimize environmental impact?

13. What role can (education/community outreach/_____) play in promoting your sustainability efforts?

14. How might you leverage (case studies/success stories/_____) to inspire innovation within your own business?

15. What steps can you take to ensure your (long-term vision/strategic planning/_____) supports both profitability and social impact?

16. What creative ways can you incentivize (employees/customers/_____) to adopt sustainable practices?

17. How can you reframe your (business challenges/resource constraints/_____) as opportunities to innovate for sustainability?

18. What actions will you take to measure the (social/environmental/_____) impact of your creative initiatives?

19. How might you adapt your (current operations/business model/_____) to meet global sustainability standards?

20. What role can (artificial intelligence/automation/_____) play in helping your business achieve sustainable innovation?

21. How could you incorporate (cultural diversity/local traditions/_____) to create inclusive, purpose-driven solutions?

22. What actions will you take to align your (corporate values/customer experience/_____) with sustainability priorities?

23. How might you use (green certifications/industry benchmarks/_____) to validate and showcase your efforts in sustainability?

24. What steps can you take to explore (alternative energy sources/low-carbon technologies/_____) in your industry?

25. How can you turn (social challenges/market disruptions/_____) into drivers of creative, sustainable innovation?

26. What creative strategies can you implement to ensure your (legacy/reputation/_____) reflects your commitment to sustainability and ethics?

21. Tech-Fueled Creativity: Leveraging Emerging Tools for Innovation

This chapter explores how technology serves as a creative ally, unlocking new possibilities for innovation in business. These questions encourage professionals to leverage tools like AI, VR, blockchain, and collaborative platforms to redefine processes, customer experiences, and value creation.

1. How can you use (AI-driven tools/machine learning/_____) to enhance your creative decision-making processes?

2. What actions will you take to integrate (blockchain/NFT technology/_____) into your value creation or ownership models?

3. How might you leverage (virtual reality/augmented reality/_____) to deliver immersive customer experiences?

4. What role can (automation/collaborative tech platforms/_____) play in streamlining your workflows creatively?

5. How could you repurpose (existing technologies/underutilized tools/_____) to solve current business challenges?

6. What steps will you take to explore (emerging trends/tech innovations/_____) for creative growth opportunities?

7. How might you integrate (data visualization tools/analytics platforms/_____) to uncover hidden patterns or insights?

8. What (collaborative apps/cloud-based solutions/_____) could you adopt to enhance team creativity and innovation?

9. How can you turn (disruptive technologies/digital disruptions/_____) into opportunities for innovation in your field?

10. What creative ways could you apply (3D printing/AI-generated content/_____) to develop new products or services?

11. How might you incorporate (wearable technology/smart devices/_____) to enrich your customer offerings?

12. What steps will you take to ensure your (technology investments/innovation projects/_____) align with your creative goals?

13. How can you use (natural language processing/chatbots/_____) to improve customer interactions or engagement?

14. What actions will you take to explore (gamification/interactivity/_____) for enhancing user experiences?

15. How might you combine (multiple technologies/cross-platform integrations/_____) to drive innovation in your business processes?

16. What (industry benchmarks/tech-based case studies/_____) can you analyze to inspire tech-fueled innovation in your business?

17. How can you leverage (AI-generated insights/automated tools/_____) to create personalized customer solutions?

18. What role could (blockchain transparency/secure digital records/_____) play in building trust with your stakeholders?

19. How might you explore (augmented reality overlays/hybrid digital-physical experiences/_____) to add depth to your brand offerings?

20. What (ethical considerations/data privacy practices/_____) must you address when integrating advanced technologies?

21. How can you train your (team/employees/_____) to use emerging tools for creativity and innovation?

22. What steps will you take to adapt your (business strategies/operational models/_____) to evolving tech landscapes?

23. How might you collaborate with (tech startups/external innovators/_____) to bring cutting-edge ideas into your business?

24. What actions can you take to integrate (automation/AI assistants/_____) into your creative problem-solving processes?

25. How could you turn (technology limitations/hardware constraints/_____) into catalysts for creative solutions?

26. What creative strategies can you implement to measure the impact of (tech innovation/new tools/_____) on your business outcomes?

22. Diversity as a Creative Catalyst

This chapter explores how diversity serves as a powerful catalyst for creativity and innovation. These questions inspire professionals to build inclusive teams, leverage global perspectives, and create environments where diverse ideas flourish and drive transformative solutions.

1. How can you create opportunities for (diverse perspectives/unconventional ideas/_____) to influence your team's problem-solving processes?

2. What steps will you take to build an (inclusive culture/collaborative environment/_____) that fosters creativity?

3. How might you leverage (global viewpoints/cultural differences/_____) to address complex challenges in your business?

4. What role can (psychological safety/open dialogue/_____) play in encouraging innovation within your diverse teams?

5. How can you use (cross-cultural collaborations/interdisciplinary approaches/_____) to inspire breakthrough ideas?

6. What actions will you take to ensure your (hiring practices/team composition/_____) embrace diversity in meaningful ways?

7. How might you reframe (team dynamics/workflows/_____) to harness the strengths of diverse talents?

8. What (training programs/resources/_____) could you implement to help your team appreciate and leverage diversity?

9. How can you encourage (mutual respect/empathy/_____) as key components of a creative and inclusive workplace?

10. What actions will you take to celebrate (individual contributions/group achievements/_____) that arise from diverse thinking?

11. How might you use (cultural traditions/global insights/_____) to enrich your product development or service offerings?

12. What steps can you take to address (biases/unconscious assumptions/_____) that hinder creativity in your organization?

13. How can you turn (language barriers/cultural misunderstandings/_____) into opportunities for collaboration and innovation?

14. What role can (diversity in leadership/inclusive decision-making/_____) play in shaping a more creative company culture?

15. How might you encourage your team to explore (new markets/underrepresented demographics/_____) with a creative lens?

16. What creative strategies can you use to highlight the value of (equity/diverse thinking/_____) in your business goals?

17. How can you design (team-building exercises/collaborative sessions/_____) that foster creative bonds across diverse groups?

18. What actions will you take to integrate (diverse customer feedback/cross-market trends/_____) into your innovation strategies?

19. How might you rethink your (workspace/environment/_____) to ensure it supports inclusion and collaboration?

20. What role can (mentorship programs/resource-sharing networks/_____) play in empowering underrepresented voices in your organization?

21. How can you measure the impact of (diverse perspectives/inclusive practices/_____) on your creative outputs?

22. What (partnerships/alliances/_____) could you build with organizations or communities to enhance diversity in your projects?

23. How might you use (storytelling/personal narratives/_____) to demonstrate the power of diversity in innovation?

24. What steps will you take to foster (curiosity/resilience/_____) in your team when working through cultural differences?

25. How can you turn (conflicting ideas/challenging conversations/_____) into opportunities for collaborative creativity?

26. What creative methods can you use to ensure that (diverse contributions/global perspectives/_____) are consistently integrated into your business strategies?

23. Business Model Innovation: Rethinking the Core of Value Creation

This chapter examines the power of business model innovation in redefining value creation. These questions encourage professionals to explore disruptive ideas, embrace iterative testing, and consider transformative models like subscriptions and platforms to drive long-term success.

1. How can you rethink your (value proposition/delivery mechanisms/_____) to create a more innovative business model?

2. What actions will you take to explore (subscription-based platforms/pay-per-use models/_____) in your industry?

3. How might you use (customer insights/market trends/_____) to identify opportunities for business model innovation?

4. What (core assumptions/existing paradigms/_____) in your business can you challenge to unlock new value?

5. How can you leverage (platform strategies/digital ecosystems/_____) to create scalable growth opportunities?

6. What role can (iterative testing/rapid prototyping/_____) play in developing and refining your business model?

7. How might you integrate (cross-industry ideas/global innovations/_____) to design a disruptive new offering?

8. What actions can you take to build (long-term customer loyalty/recurring revenue streams/_____) through innovative models?

9. How can you turn (competitive threats/market disruptions/_____) into catalysts for transforming your business structure?

10. What creative strategies could you employ to align your (pricing models/service tiers/_____) with evolving customer needs?

11. How might you use (collaborative partnerships/strategic alliances/_____) to enhance your value creation processes?

12. What steps will you take to evaluate the (sustainability/scalability/_____) of a potential new business model?

13. How can you incorporate (customer feedback/performance metrics/_____) into your innovation process for business models?

14. What (technology trends/digital tools/_____) could you leverage to create a groundbreaking business framework?

15. How might you redefine your (target audience/revenue streams/_____) to better fit an innovative model?

16. What actions can you take to turn (one-time purchases/customer touchpoints/_____) into continuous engagement opportunities?

17. How can you adapt your (supply chain/operational workflows/_____) to support a more agile business model?

18. What (case studies/success stories/_____) from other industries can inspire you to rethink your business structure?

19. How might you use (network effects/customer communities/_____) to amplify the impact of your business model?

20. What creative ways can you test (low-risk pilot projects/experimental frameworks/_____) for new business ideas?

21. How can you balance (innovation/risk management/_____) when transitioning to a disruptive business model?

22. What steps will you take to ensure your (value creation/customer relationships/_____) remain at the core of your business transformation?

23. How might you design (flexible revenue streams/multi-sided platforms/_____) to future-proof your business?

24. What actions can you take to identify and address (barriers/resistance/_____) to implementing a new business model?

25. How can you evaluate the (long-term viability/competitive advantages/_____) of the innovative models you're considering?

26. What creative methods can you employ to align your (team culture/organizational goals/_____) with your business model evolution?

24. Creativity Metrics: Measuring and Sustaining Innovation

This chapter focuses on quantifying creativity to drive sustainable innovation. These questions explore metrics, tools, and strategies that help businesses measure the impact of creative efforts, balance ROI, and build accountability into their long-term innovation initiatives.

1. How can you measure the (time-to-market/implementation success/_____) of your creative initiatives?

2. What steps will you take to define (key performance indicators/impact metrics/_____) for your innovation efforts?

3. How might you assess the (short-term ROI/long-term value/_____) of a creative project?

4. What actions can you take to track the (adoption rates/employee engagement/_____) resulting from your creative strategies?

5. How can you use (feedback loops/real-time data/_____) to refine your metrics for innovation success?

6. What role can (qualitative insights/quantitative metrics/_____) play in evaluating the impact of your creativity?

7. How might you incorporate (customer feedback/team input/_____) into measuring creative outcomes?

8. What steps can you take to align your (creative goals/business objectives/_____) with measurable results?

9. How could you balance (financial metrics/creative freedom/_____) when evaluating innovative projects?

10. What tools will you use to track the (cost efficiency/value creation/_____) of your creative initiatives?

11. How can you measure the (cultural impact/employee satisfaction/_____) of fostering creativity in your organization?

12. What metrics might you create to gauge (idea generation/problem-solving effectiveness/_____) across your teams?

13. How can you measure the success of (collaborative brainstorming/innovation sessions/_____) in driving tangible outcomes?

14. What (benchmarking practices/industry comparisons/_____) can you use to assess your creativity against competitors?

15. How might you evaluate the (longevity/scalability/_____) of an innovative idea?

16. What actions can you take to ensure that (sustainability/ethical impact/_____) are integrated into your creative metrics?

17. How can you measure the (risk-reward balance/strategic value/_____) of exploring disruptive ideas?

18. What creative strategies will you use to balance (exploration/execution/_____) in measuring innovation progress?

19. How might you adapt your (measurement tools/analysis frameworks/_____) to changing market conditions?

20. What steps can you take to track (team contributions/individual creativity/_____) during the development process?

21. How can you use (predictive analytics/data-driven insights/_____) to forecast the impact of your creative initiatives?

22. What metrics could you design to evaluate the (customer experience/customer loyalty/_____) improvements driven by innovation?

23. How might you assess the (speed of iteration/frequency of experimentation/_____) in your creative processes?

24. What (surveys/feedback mechanisms/_____) can you implement to gauge the perceived value of your creative efforts?

25. How will you measure the (long-term cultural shifts/organizational learning/_____) resulting from sustained creativity?

26. What actions will you take to ensure that your (creative investments/measurement strategies/_____) remain adaptable and impactful over time?

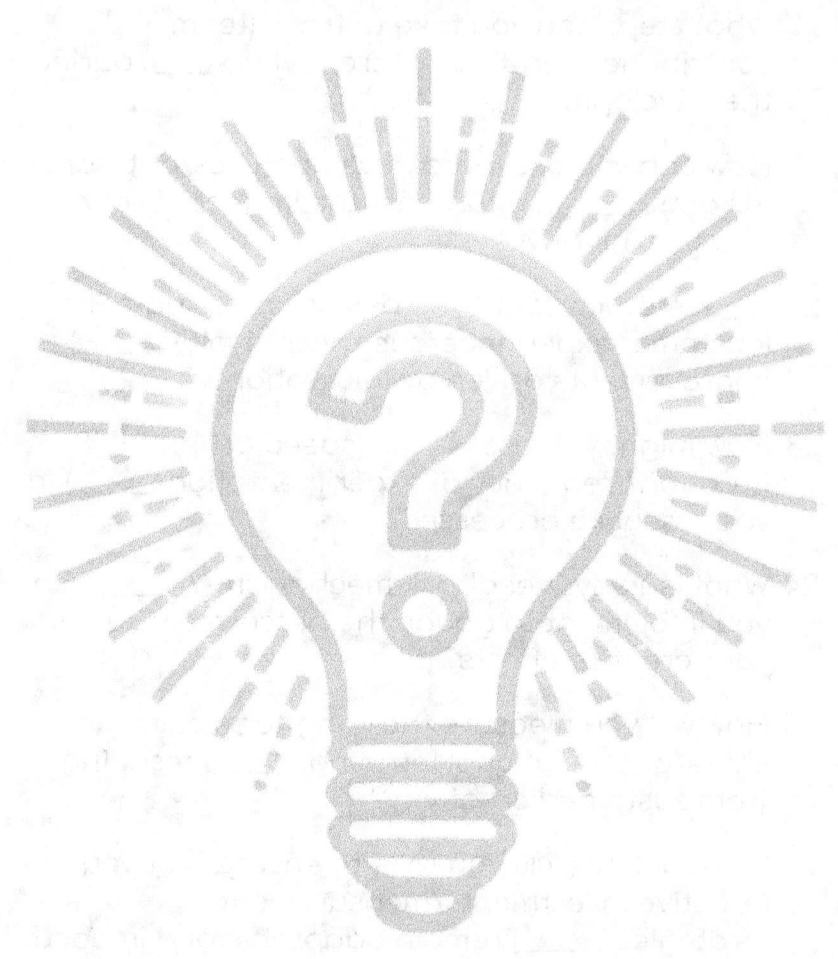

Share Your Wisdom

Thank you for joining me on this journey to ignite creativity and unlock new opportunities in business. I hope this book has sparked fresh ideas and provided valuable insights that you can carry forward in your work.

Now, I invite you to share your wisdom with others. By sharing your thoughts about this book, you can help inspire fellow professionals to embrace creativity and innovation in their own journeys. Your feedback has the power to guide others toward transformative ideas and solutions.

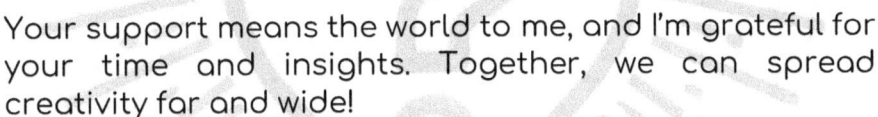

To do so, please scan this QR code.

Your support means the world to me, and I'm grateful for your time and insights. Together, we can spread creativity far and wide!

Thank you.

Mauricio

About the Author

Mauricio Vasquez is an accomplished business strategist, creativity advocate, and thought leader with over 20 years of international experience spanning the mining, power, and renewable energy sectors. His expertise in business strategy, risk management, and insurance has helped organizations across Canada, the US, Latin America, and the Caribbean navigate challenges, uncover opportunities, and drive impactful results.

As a Senior Vice President at a leading risk management firm, Mauricio specializes in helping companies achieve their corporate objectives while enhancing resilience and preserving value. His multifaceted career has included leadership roles in risk control engineering, insurance, enterprise risk management, and client executive advisory, all of which have sharpened his ability to craft creative solutions tailored to complex business landscapes.

Mauricio is also an accomplished author, having published books on creativity, coaching, and leadership, including *555 Powerful Questions in Coaching, Mentoring and Leading at Work* and *555 Powerful AI Prompts for Coaching, Mentoring, and Leadership Mastery in Business*. His passion for personal and professional growth extends to his entrepreneurial ventures, including co-founding *Aria Capri*, a brand focused on promoting positivity and resilience for children.

With certifications in enterprise risk management and coaching, alongside specialized training in artificial intelligence from MIT, Mauricio bridges the worlds of innovation, strategy, and creativity. Fluent in Spanish and English, he is deeply committed to fostering global perspectives and inspiring others to think boldly and creatively in every aspect of their work.

In this book, Mauricio invites you to embark on a transformative journey of discovery, providing 555 thought-provoking questions to unlock creativity, overcome challenges, and achieve innovation-driven growth.

For more about Mauricio and his work, visit his LinkedIn profile: https://www.linkedin.com/in/mauriciovasquez/

www.ingramcontent.com/pod-product-compliance
Lightning Source LLC
Chambersburg PA
CBHW071105120626
46546CB00003B/1281